Leather Projects

A pictorial guide

Copyright © 2011 Paul Carpenter

Learn how to:

Use leather stamping tools

Carve basic patterns into leather

Use and prep Rawhide and Leather lace to make a braided quiver and covering for a knife handle with fid work and pineapple knots.

Published by Lulu.com

ISBN number 978-1-4478-8431-6

Other publications by Paul Carpenter

Travel;

Six Mountain hikes from around the World

The Moray way and the Ben Macdui Trail

Crafts;

Leather and Wood Crafts

The leather lace Bullwhip

Leather Armour

Bows and Arrows, Homemade

Contents

As always, the procedures outlined within this book you do at your own risk.

Caution – if you do use axes, power tools and other potentially dangerous tools, make sure you know how to use them i.e. how to stand/hold/cut with them – it's the wood your trying to cut not you or anybody else – use of apparatus (which make bow making easier and safer) such as shave Horse.

Leather Stamping a design on a quiver

Tools and stamp tools used –x503, x511, x688, x507

Plus dyeing of lace and leather. Edge burnishing, lacing holes and edge braid.

Finished article – using different stamp patterns, edge braid and colouring to decorate a quiver

Tools

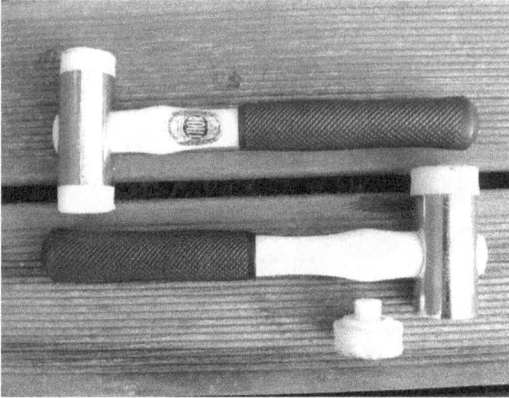

Soft rubber hammers with replaceable heads and illustration of the stamp tools used

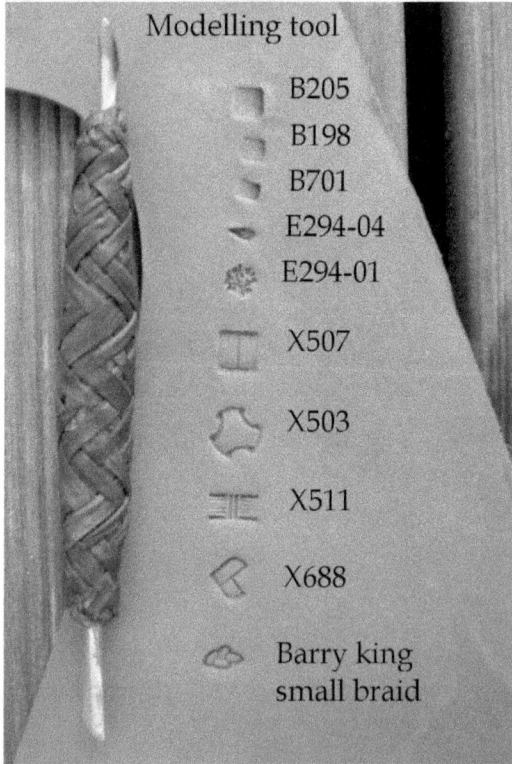

Modelling tool

B205

B198

B701

E294-04

E294-01

X507

X503

X511

X688

Barry king small braid

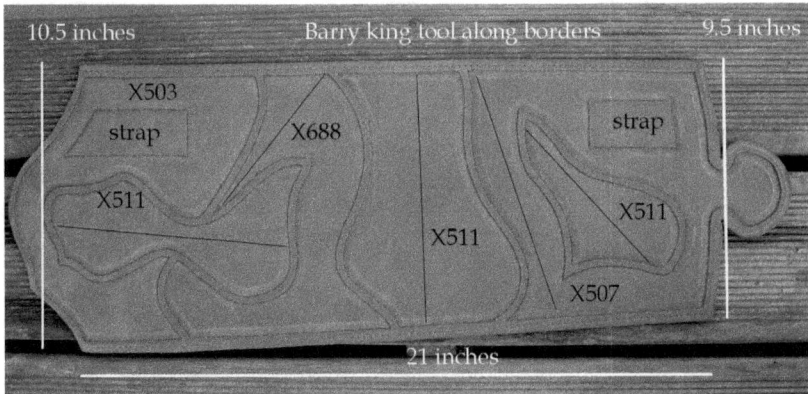

Placement of tools shown on cut and bevelled leather quiver pattern – thin black lines are positions of tooling guide lines (non needed for X503) – marking and cutting of braid holes along edge are shown at the end. Both the decorative stamps E294 are used around the edges once the main stamping is done.

X503

Being a geometric tool, guidelines are needed and there is a variety of ways to place them to make different pattern. After some experimentation I came up with what is shown on the proceeding pages which is a repeating pattern based on six stamps making a circle creating a five sided concave shape within them. I am not the best when it come to spending time setting out guide lines and for this pattern I stamped one impression then gently marked the places for the next five, then stamped them once the desired shape match up.

Different patterns require matching up at different parts of stamp – with this one you can see above how I matched each proceeding stamp to one another.

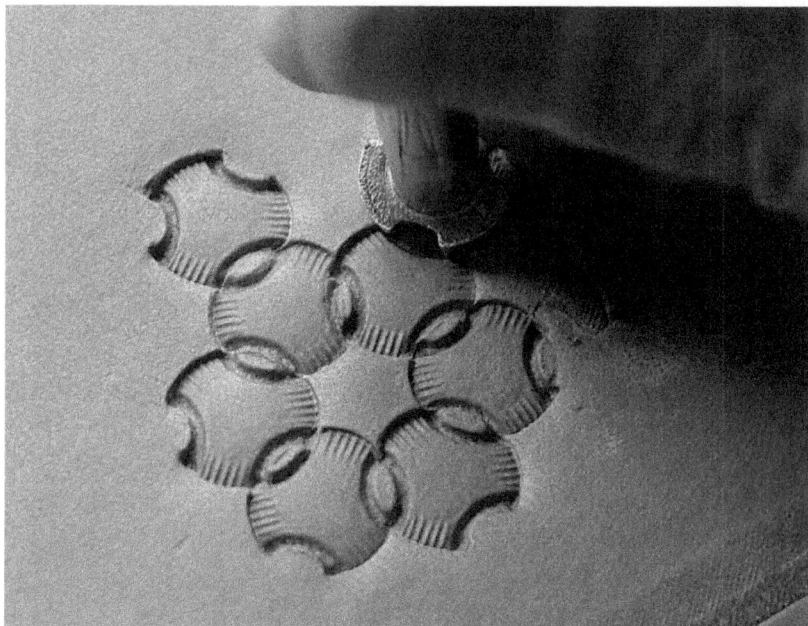

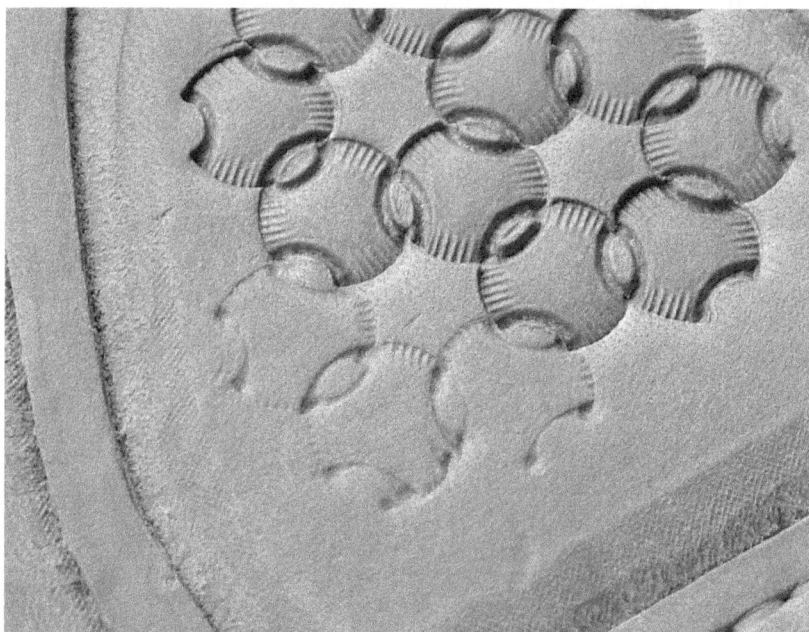

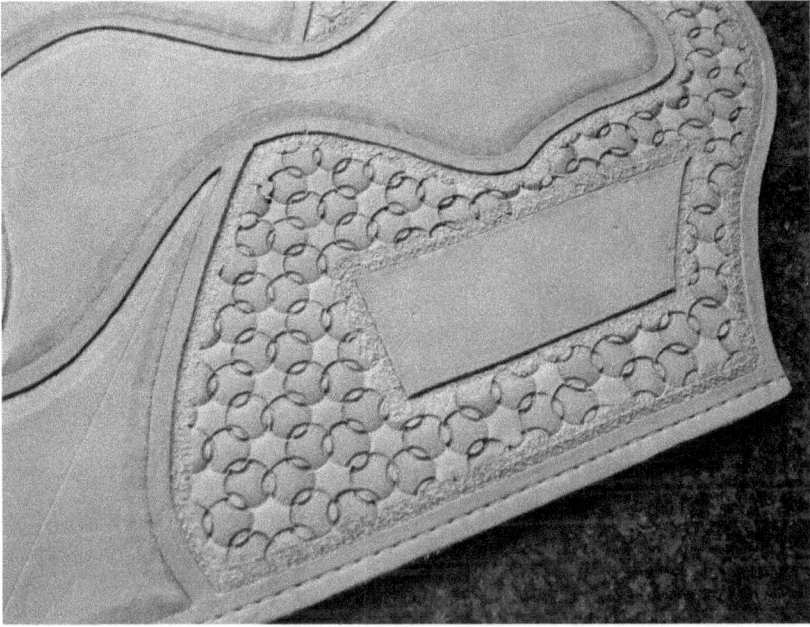

Above shows some of the pattern finished – if you look carefully you're probably see a multitude of places where I messed up but the overall appearance is still looking good.

X511

Arrow pattern – Again this tool can be used to make numerous patterns, but the guidelines to starting are similar. The object of gently marking the first course as seen below is to ensure they all lay correct to one another. Basically the first mark is taken from the central guide line, the next impression (whether placed below or above the first – your preference) is also laid on the centre line with the tail end of it overlapping the tail end of the first impression, as shown by the circle. From there on you should have two positions i.e. the centre line and a tail end – to help position the next impression.

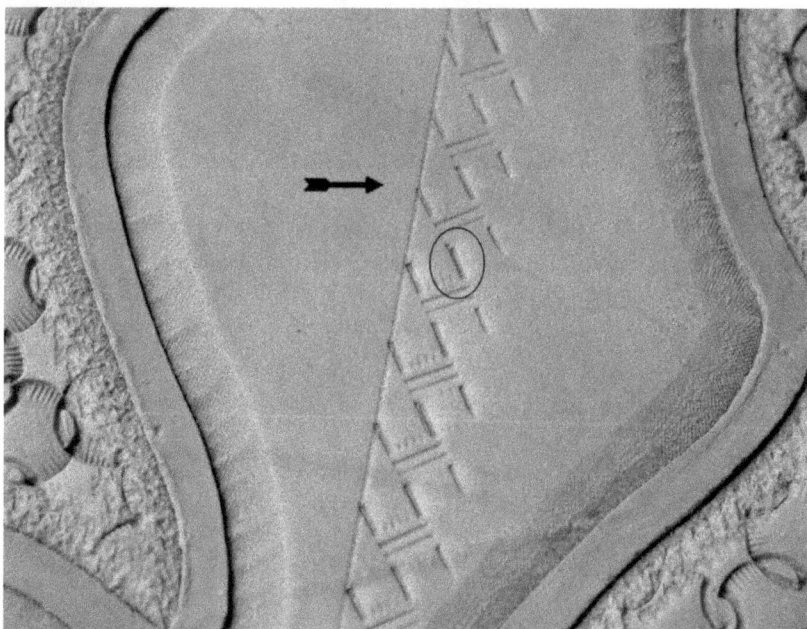

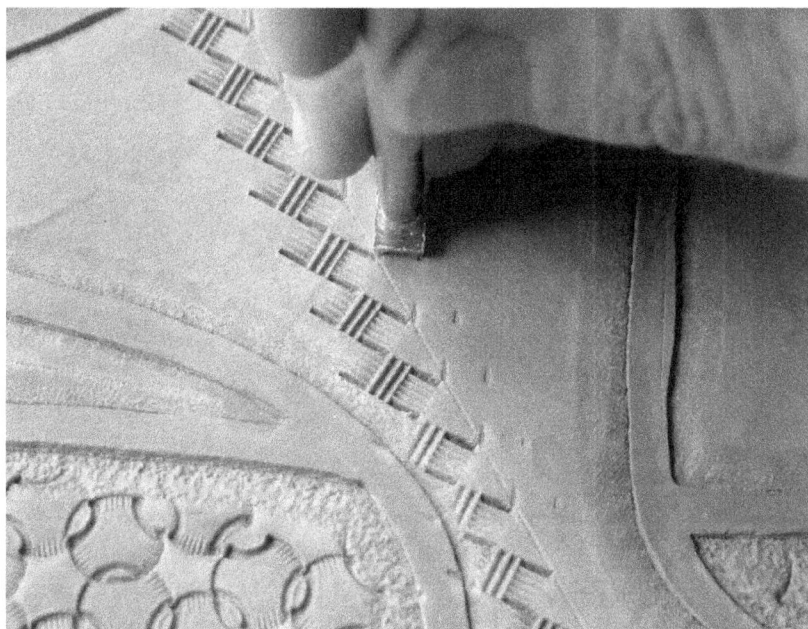

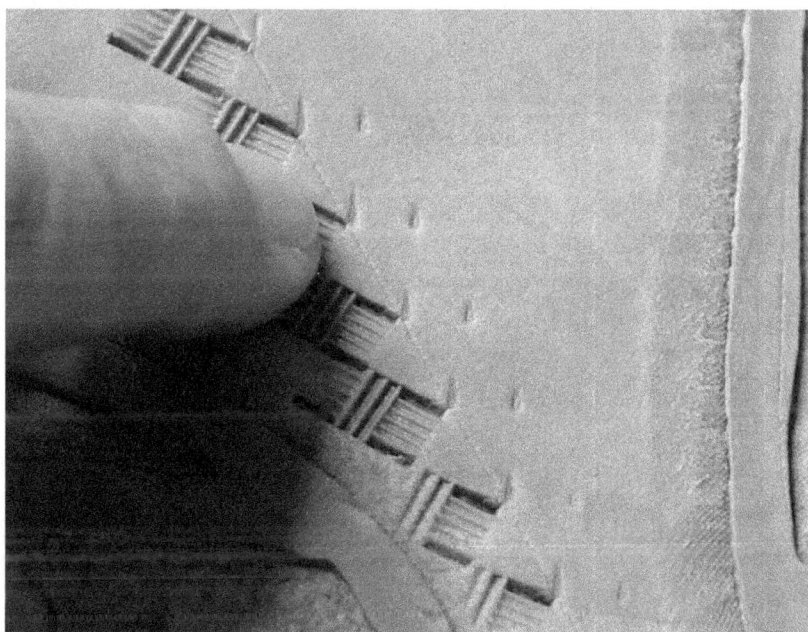

After you have stamped the first line, then you make marks for laying the opposite line of stamps which run in a mirror image opposite to the first using again the centre line and the tail ends as reference points and also the end points of the opposite stamp.

Above just shows the actual stamping paying care that all reference points match up as good as possible.

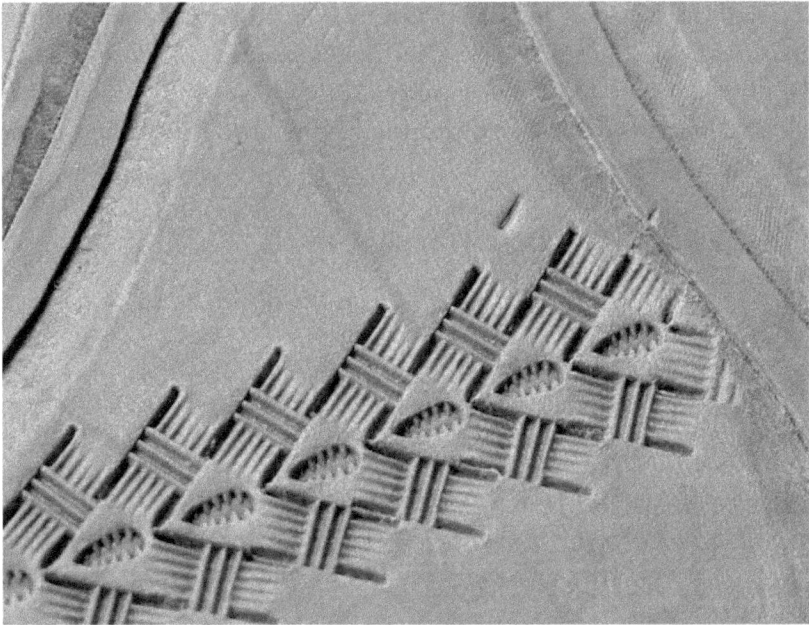

To start of change of the stamp pattern from an arrow to just straight runs. As seen in the photo below, the first impassion is made at one end by matching up with the outer tail end. From there after stamping that initial stamp it is just a case of matching up the two tail ends as shown below.

This shows the continuation of matching up tail ends and placing guides

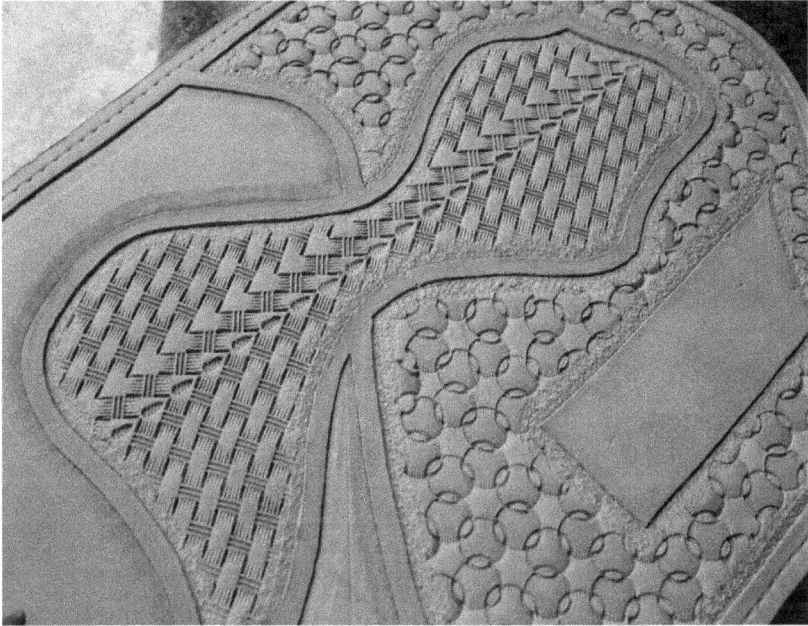

This photo show the completed pattern produced with two central arrow pattern. The choice of whether you want the arrow or straight line patterns will dictate where you place the guide stamps and once you start and look at the developing patterns, these or the best start position for you will become apparent. I am left handed so where I find it best to start may not be the same for all you righties – Make sure you keep looking at the whole pattern as it develops as the slight miss-placement of stamps can cause straight lines to curve, as can be seen below left in the photo above. Because this pattern involved overlapping the tail ends of the stamp, these slight curves can be accommodated slightly but do make any finished article a bit off - I did it deliberately of course just as an example!!!! You will notice that I used Tandy tool F872 in the centre arrows, this was to aid hiding the guide line.

X688

This is not one of the easiest tools to make patterns with but the effect is OK. As with the last tool an initial central line is used to do a first line of impressions lining the line up with the V of the stamp – again lay guide marks first then go over doing the proper stamps.

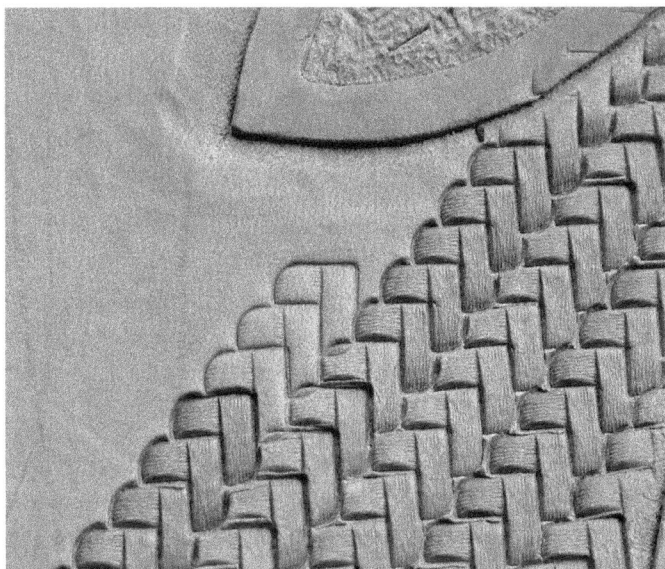

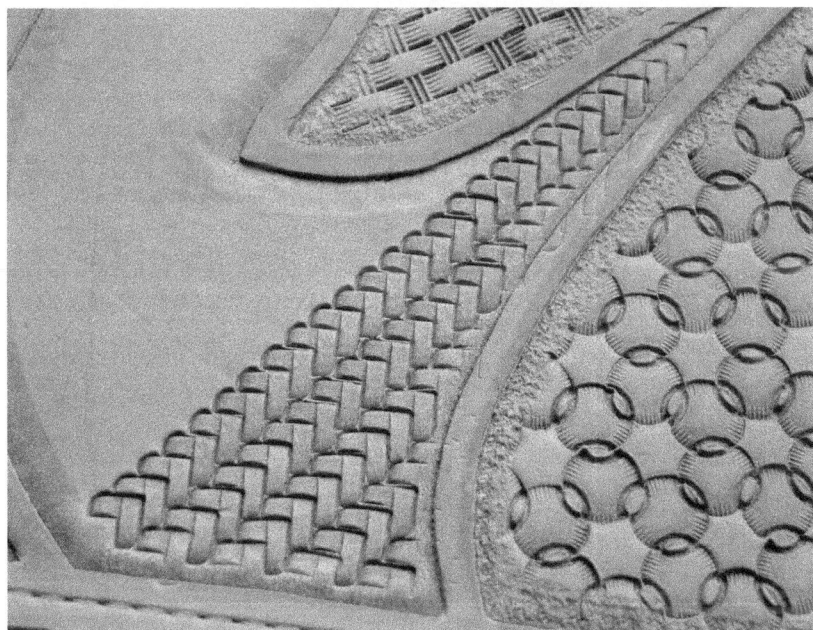

The proceeding photos photo show a section of the tooling finished – upon stamping the rest of the area, there was a severe curve that developed as misplacing of the stamp is easy here having only one very slight matching position that can be used to match up adjoining stamps. You can also see how the decorative tools E294 are used along the edge of each stamped pattern.

X507

X507 is probably one of the better known basket weave tools. As normal an initial guide line is placed and then the tool is stamped using alternative sides to produce the basket weave effect. As can be seen from my efforts, it is remarkably easy to place each stamp slightly wrong.

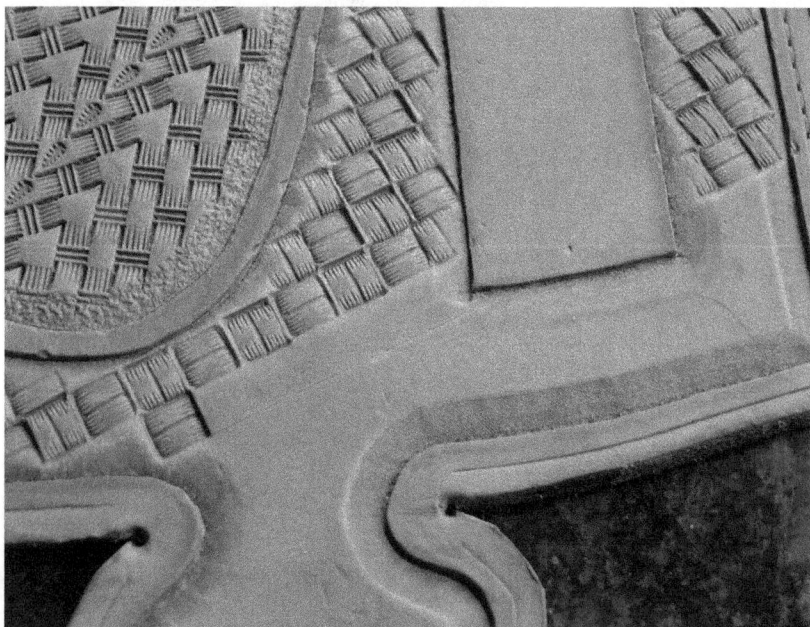

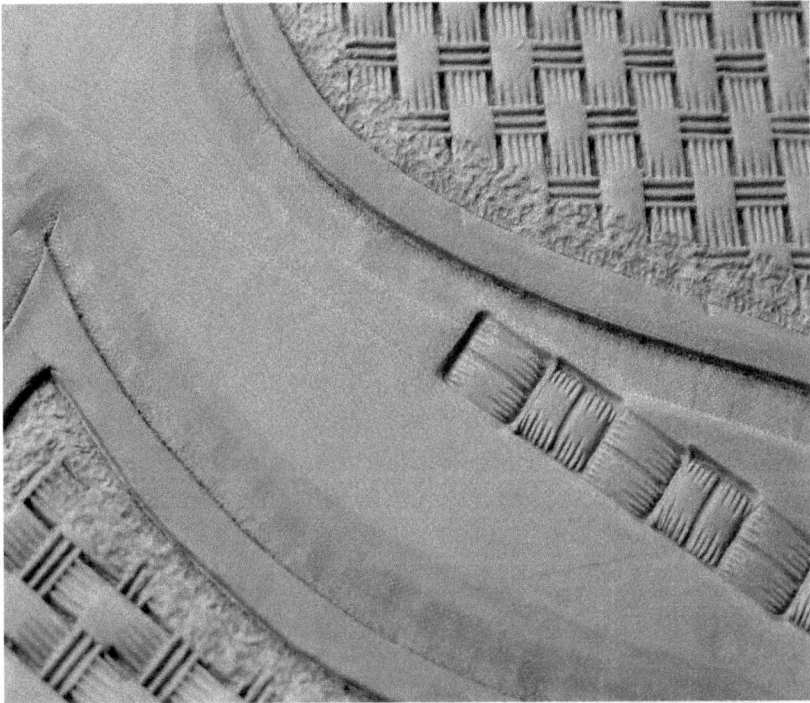

Although for once I did not do the worse mistake and that is to fail to turn the tool or otherwise stamp the same two directions of the tool in a line, unfortunately this does show up really easily. The only way to try and change it is re-stamp one of the two again the right way but really hard then use the modelling tool to try and smooth the wrong lines out. It is also quite easy to start the curve effect of the lines; the only way to prevent this is to continually lay more guide lines as shown in the right photo.

The last two photos show the completed stamps – you will notice the use of Barry kings tool on the borders of each stamp – plus you may notice the curves (intentional one's of course) from some of the stamping patterns and how each tool pattern matches up even whilst tooled around objects.

Lace and leather prep, dyeing and braid

Tools

S is my half round knife which I use for skiving, plus an old chisel grinded down to use to cut slits for 6mm lace and lastly the 5 to an inch overstitcher marker.

Here is a small clamp I bought from weaver which I find great for prepping lace, a pair of pliers to aid pulling slippery lace, a cheap craft knife with disposable snap off blades – sharp enough for the job and no time wasting sharpening. Lastly the **Osborne scratch awl**.

Leather prep – making lacing holes

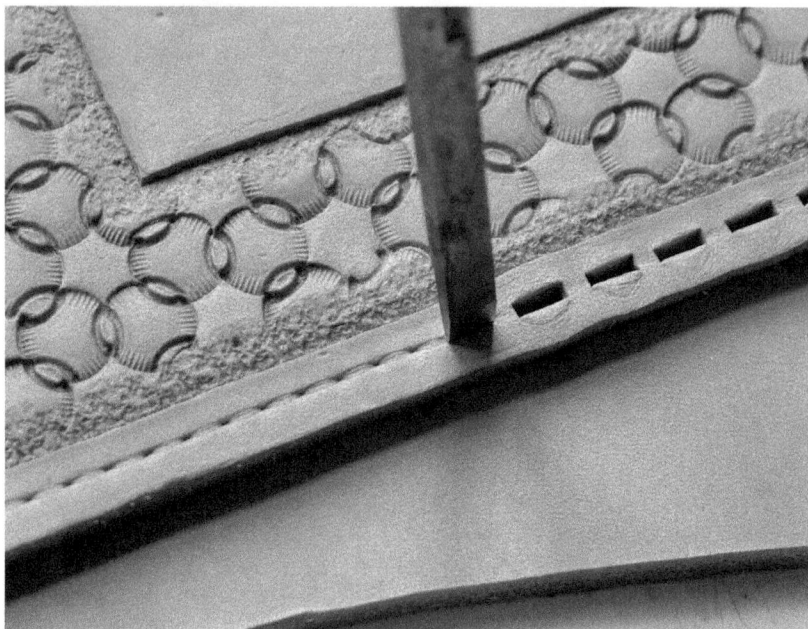

First used a divider to mark a thin line down the edge of the leather, and then ran the 5 to 1 inch overstitcher along that line. Starting with the top first sewing indent lay the hole cutter as shown – width of this cutter means that it is perfectly spaced between the sewing hole indents. Use a soft hammer to hammer chisel into leather and ensure you have a spare piece of leather underneath to protect cutter edge. Most important each side's hole should match up for braiding, ensure this by starting the holes an equal distance from the top of the leather.

Around the bottom of the quiver, the lace needs to be braided so that it is hidden and not liable to be nicked/broken by arrow heads, skiving the underside edge slightly after making the holes ensures they are.

After the holes have been made and dyeing, use the scratch awl to open up the underside of the holes to aid braiding – do this very delicately, you only need to push it into the holes gently – too hard and you could break the leather on thinner wetter leather.

Edge burnishing

Once the edges are edged this is how they start out, rough and ragged.

There are many ways to edge leather with all sort of dyes, solutions –
After countless disasters, I tend now to just use water and canvas. For
this method just wet the edge slightly then rub with the canvas (black
canvas shown here)

This is the end result after rubbing for a minute, rubbing for longer produces a nicer glass sheen – I use this method mostly on saddle horn edges.

Dyeing and coating lace

A photo of my dyeing set up ready for dyeing. Includes dye bottles, shearling used in spreading the dye, lace bevelled and cut to length needed, plus Aussie conditioner to lubricate and set dye, and disposable gloves. All of this is put onto a plastic bag and another sheet of thicker plastic is laid on the floor to catch any drips and to ensure that the lace does not pick up any debris from the floor.

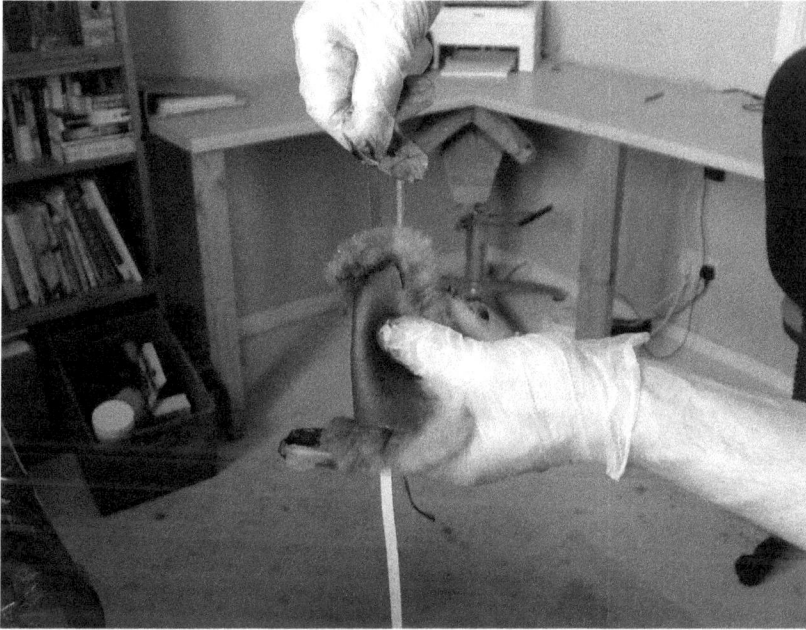

Pour some dye onto the shearling, fold this around the lace and pull.
Pour more dye when undyed patches appear on the lace, and run the lace
through the shearling from the other end to ensure edges are dyed.

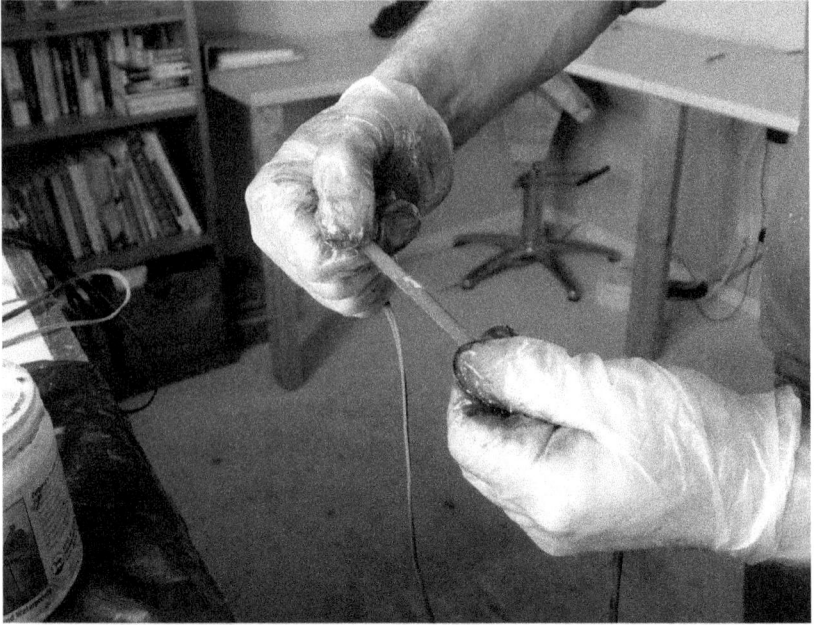

With the Aussie conditioner you are trying to coat the front and back of the lace in the wax. First, rub a little into the gloves, which help to bind the dye on them. Do not use neat's-foot oil on lace – it tends to weaken it.

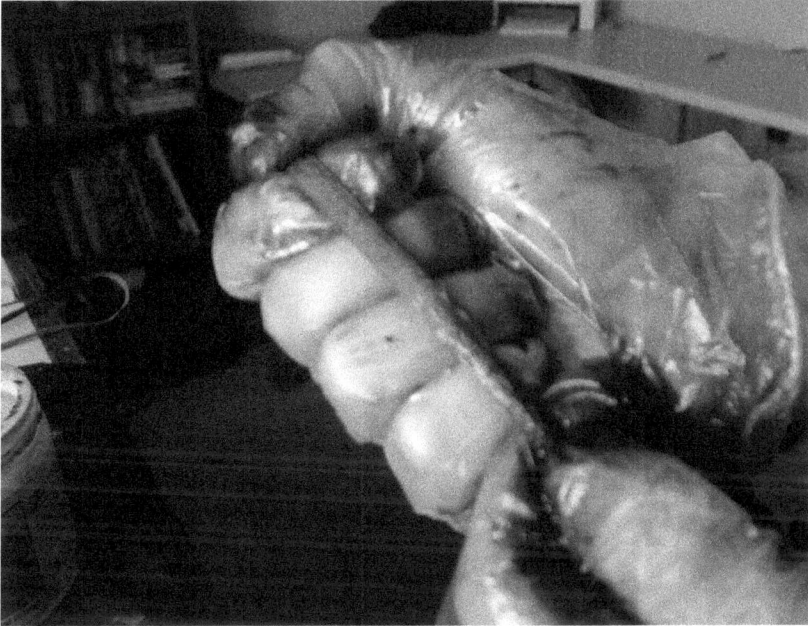

Here you can see the look of the lace on the back once covered in Aussie conditioner – you should keep checking that it has soaked into the rear, as it tends not to catch as easily on the rear as it does the front

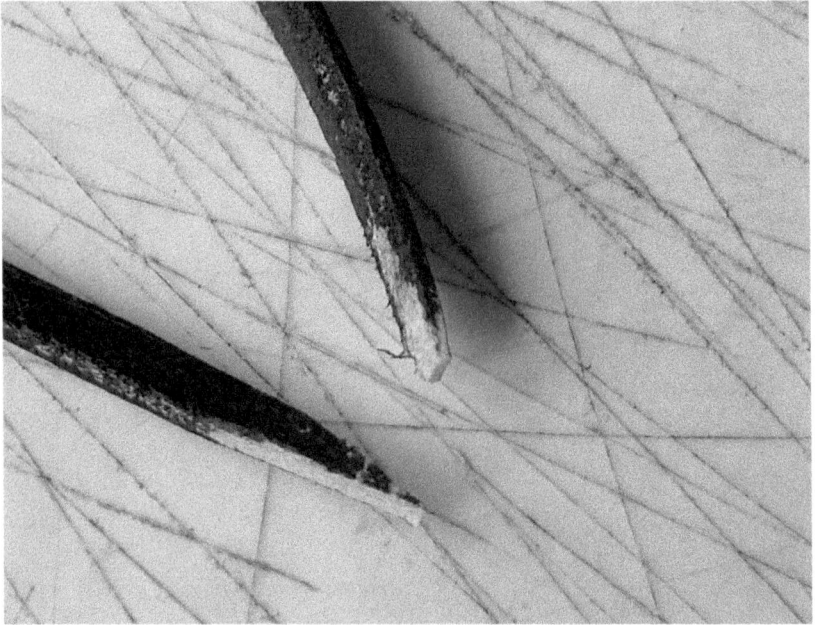

I use the 2 prong lacing needles – first cut the tip of the lace to a V, then slightly skive the end. Open up the needle, push in the lace and fasten tight with the pliers.

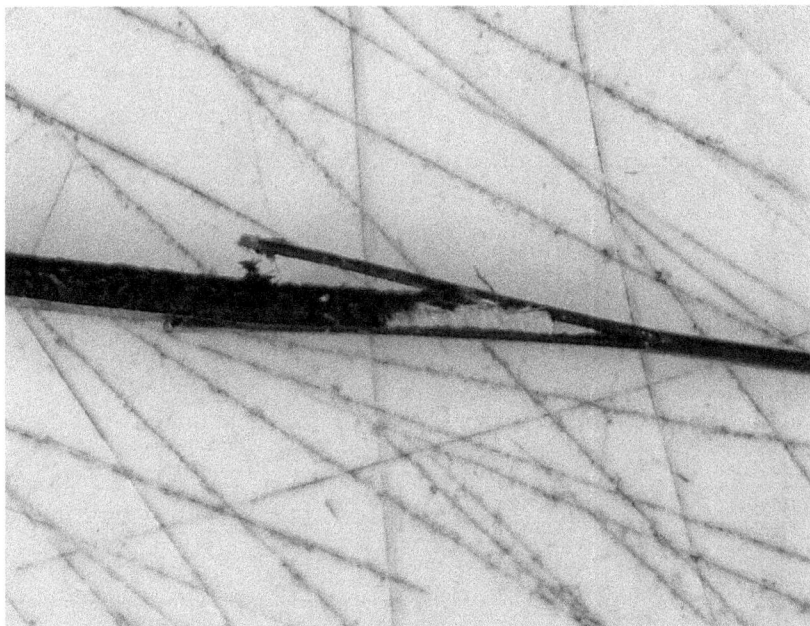

Lace fastened into needle and ready to go.

Edge braid

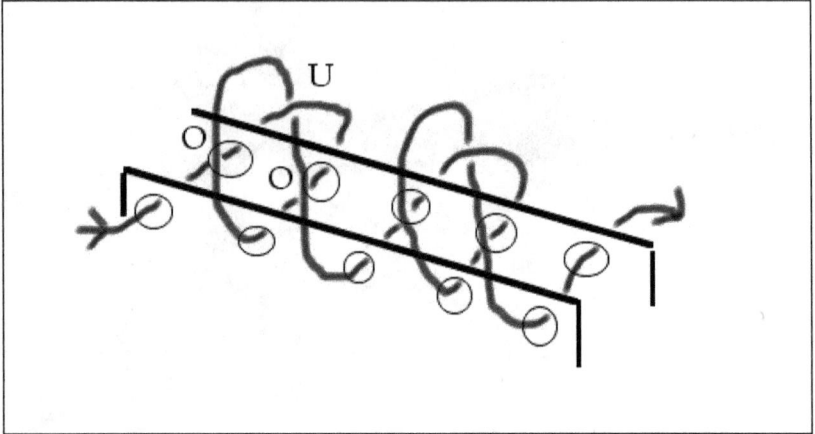

(don't do this stage until a strap is sewn in place) The photo above explains the main braid I used down the long edge of the quiver – For this sort of item I prefer the edge braids that only need to go into the holes once. O denotes over and U denotes under. The braid is basically two loops either side of the edges which are looped into one another – during this looping the lace will have to be twisted back on itself to ensure that the front shows and not the back – it's not too duffercult. Because the main leather I used was fairly thick I needed tie lace at various locations along the length of the edge to help keep it together, but it also helps to take up the tension in trying to keep the edges together as you try to braid. The finished produced should see the leather edges resting edge on edge but the only way to first braid this edge was to tie the edge side on side allowing the needle to be pushed from one side to the other – this is OK, once finished just push both sides of the edging down gently. When using thinner leather for such a project such as 5 -7 oz, you can allow the leather to completely dry and should still have no problem bending it into shape but because the

36

leather I used was more 10 – 12oz I needed to braid while the leather was still damp – there is no problem with this but you should watch that the stamping does not fade.

Dyeing leather

For dyeing I have a similar set up as I do for the lace, except in this case I plan to cover the whole of the leather in a solution of neat's-foot oil with antique stain mixed into it plus some dye of the same colour. After applying this I used a cotton bud (normally used to clean ears with) soaked in dye to create the streaks over the leather at various positions. Lastly going over this all with the shearling again to blend it all together – I am not sure what effect I was after but I think it looks good as a sort of camouflage, ideal for quivers. After dyeing, I coated both sides in Aussie conditioner and left it to soak for a few hours.

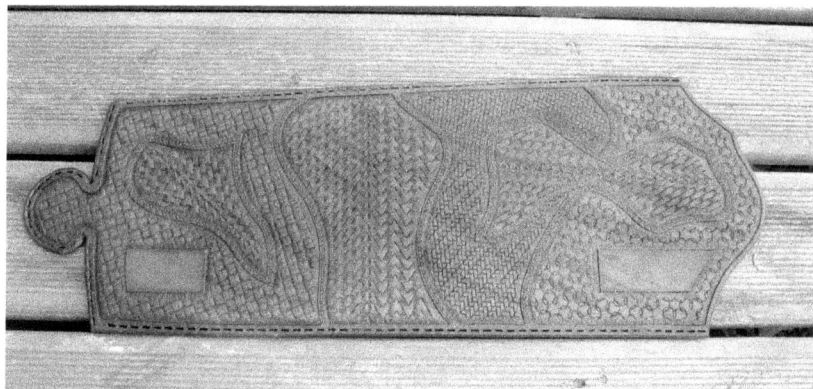

Leather dyed and finished ready for lacing

Leather carving a simple design into a belt

The designs shown here are quite simple but the methods used can be used are similar to those of other Celtic or tribal designs.

Covered here is; pictures, Initial carving, Tooling and modeling, eliminating tool marks and painting.

Initial Carving - This is a picture of the set up I use. But first the pattern I choose was transferred onto draft paper or tracing paper. Next the leather (once cut out to the shape needed) is soaked in warm water and left in a plastic bag to allow the water to soak throughout the hide for an hour to overnight (depending on the amount and thickness).When the leather is ready (i.e. the leathers surface colour is near to its original but still soft), the design is transferred onto the leather and the cut marks made. I used two different knives to cut with, the filigree and a narrow square edge. The leather they are placed on is my sharpening tool – basically any veg tanned leather with an abrasive compound rubbed onto it – the main purpose of this is to keep the edge and bevel smooth which I use throughout the cutting process, i.e. when the blade starts to drag, run it a few times both sides over the compound.

Reference my table top. The white surface is thin plastic board which lies over a thick large marble stone that I gathered from a stone mason down the road. It enables me to have a large cutting and work area in the same area, plus tooling and carving on the same bench.

Tooling and modelling each segment

The following series of photos show the process of bevelling the areas needed to be pushed in (carved leather is not carved as such but more indented). The B stamping tools are used for this (B for bevel) using which ever width of tool you feel is appropriate for the item to be bevelled.

There numerous methods of bevelling, each more appropriate to the crafter – below is just the way I do it but is no means the best – experimentation is the only way you find your way.

First one side is bevelled – due to the narrow piece being bevelled I held the tool at an angle to avoid as much as possible, indentation of it on the other side of the leather.

Next the other side is bevelled.

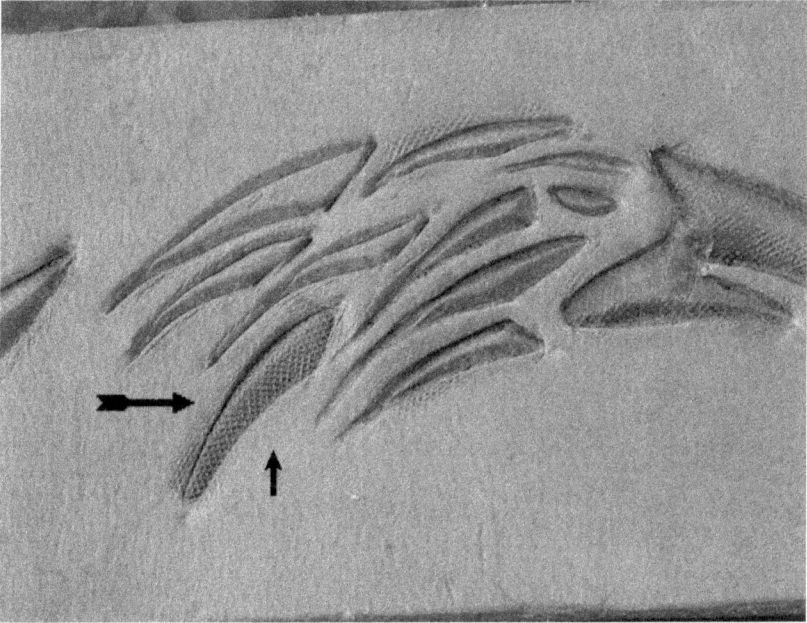

Then re-bevel each side more gently to further push the leather down.

Lastly use a modelling tool to further establish the desired effect by pushing the whole area down to a uniform depth.

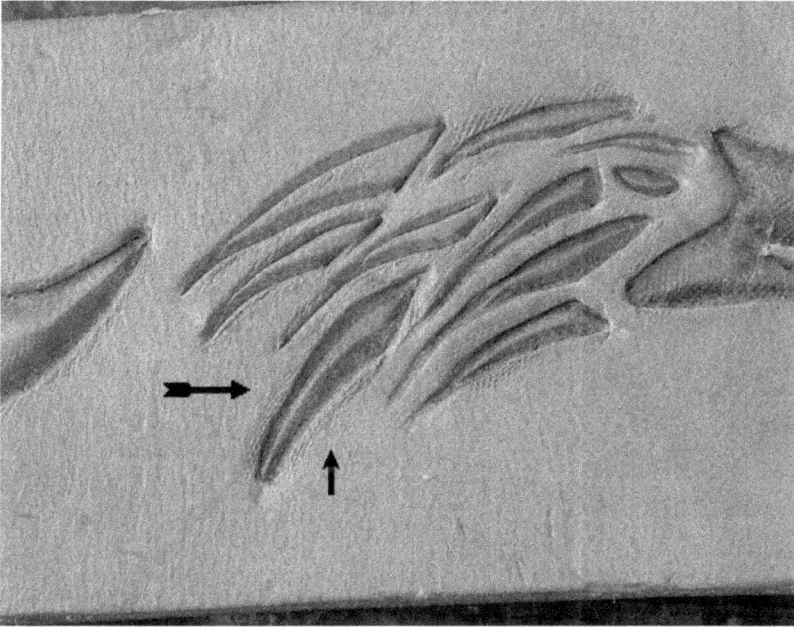

finished and ready to go onto the next part – in this instance the depth that the carving goes down to is not very deep only about 3mm – for larger areas this could be deeper (some estimate that a depth of ¾ the thickness of the leather is best). I carved shallow here due to the small area's being tooled.

Procedure of eliminating tool marks

The next photos show the process of leaving a smooth tooled edge when using the B tools. The modelling tool can eliminate some of these but when the leather is getting on the dry side you could be left with rough ugly marks.

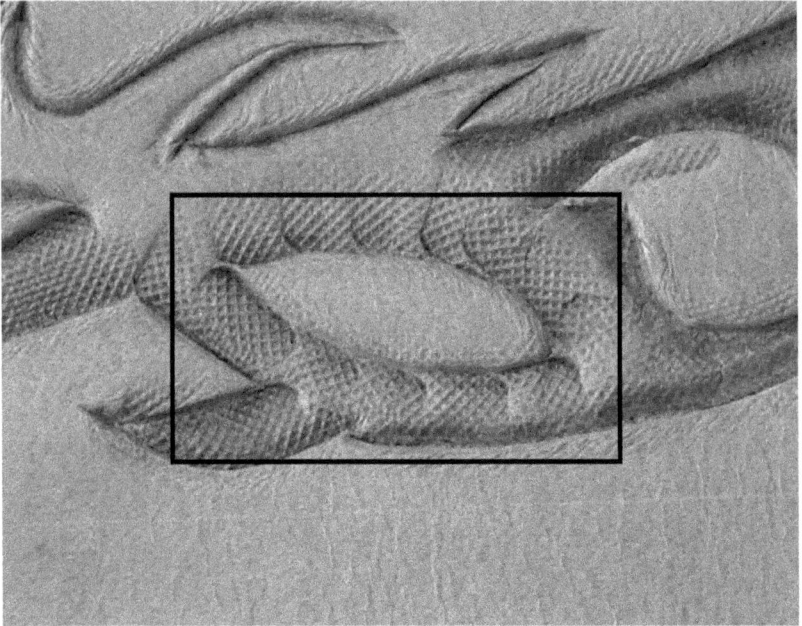

This is how the leather looks after just going around the edge with a B tool showing the rough edge.

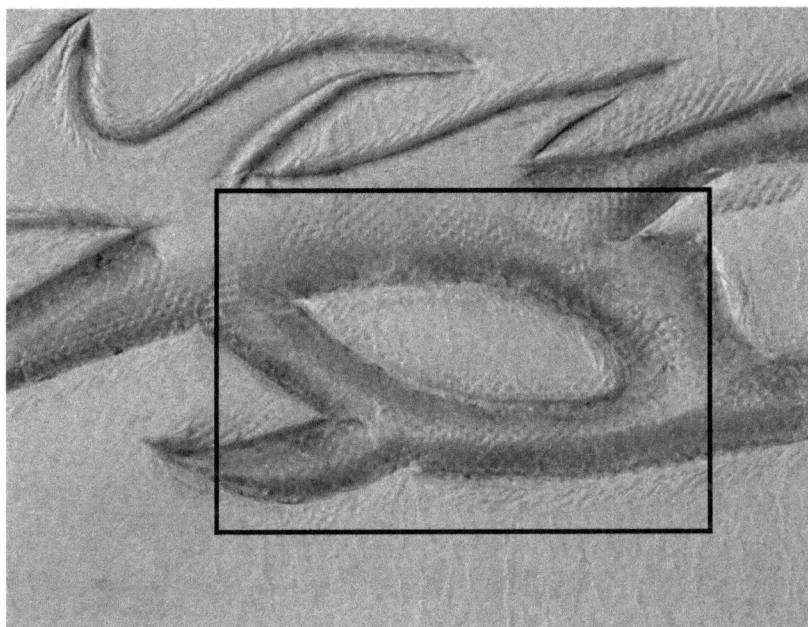

After the initial stamping of the edge, go over the edge again with the B tool but not pushing down as hard. This helps even out the tooled edge.

The very narrow points of an area are always difficult to get exact – I use the modelling tool in the way shown to define a sharp edge – it is not a perfect method but experience will again produce better results.

This photo shows the completed tooled image – on some outer edges can still be seen the imprints of the B tools, these in wet leather can just be smoothed out by running the flat side of the modelling tool over then lightly.

Painted

For a item like this, I like to dye the main pattern to help it stand out better, the photo below shows the thinness of brush I use - I basically got a thin brush then cut about half the bristle off until I was happy with the end result.

Once the belt was finished and dyed I coated it in neat's-foot – let that dry over night then applied another layer with green dye added into it – the two won't mix to well but enough to give a faded effect of the colour added. Antique Stain tends to mix better with neat's-foot oil if you'd prefer to try that and gives a much better uniform colour

Making a woven Rawhide back Quiver

I started making rawhide quivers years ago when I had started to make rawhide primarily to back bows with. At that time my experience with braiding and lace in general was very little and found this project fairly easy as it does not require alot of the lace/lace prep that other rawhide projects need. This quiver could hold upto 15 arrows.

You could use almost any material to make these quivers along as that material can hold its shape once finished. For the rawhide, this is achieved by the stiffness created by dry rawhide plus the varnish that is applied to make it damp proof, or so that it does not turn into a slobby mess in a down pour of rain. As with my other tutorials, please bear in mind that I am left handed, so some instruction may need to be reversed to make sense. Also, please read the whole tutorial before starting.

Prep of rawhide - Cutting out laces - Amounts of lace needed, soaking/dyeing rawhide - Cutting the mould - laying the vertical laces - Braiding the quiver –Shoulder strap - Drying – Fixing on the top – waterproofing.

This is the finished quiver holding a dozen arrows.

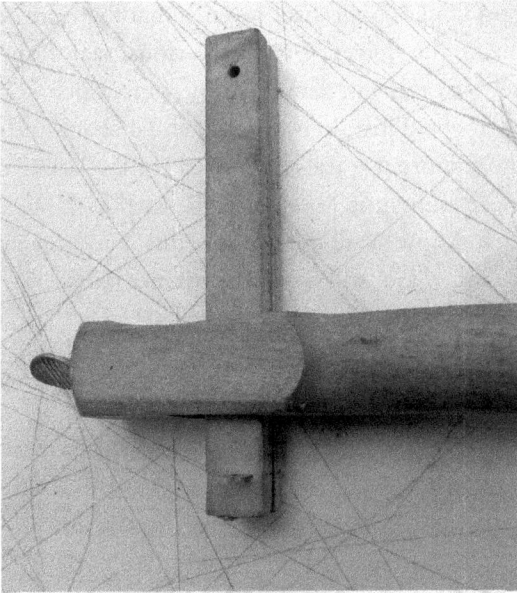
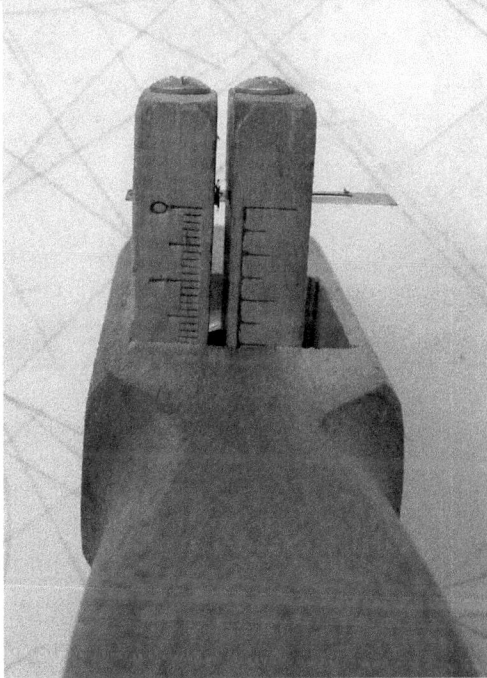

One of the good things about this project is that there are very little tools you need to make the quiver. On the previous page I show a wooden type lace cutter you can buy from **Tandy** with which you will cut the rawhide. Or you could just do it by hand and a sharp knife as I used to do – there is no importance really in a need for the laces or lace to be of equal width, near enough is good enough for this. Note the width the cutter is set to and how small the gap is – this is to prevent the rawhide wrinkling up to much as it will do on the thinner parts.

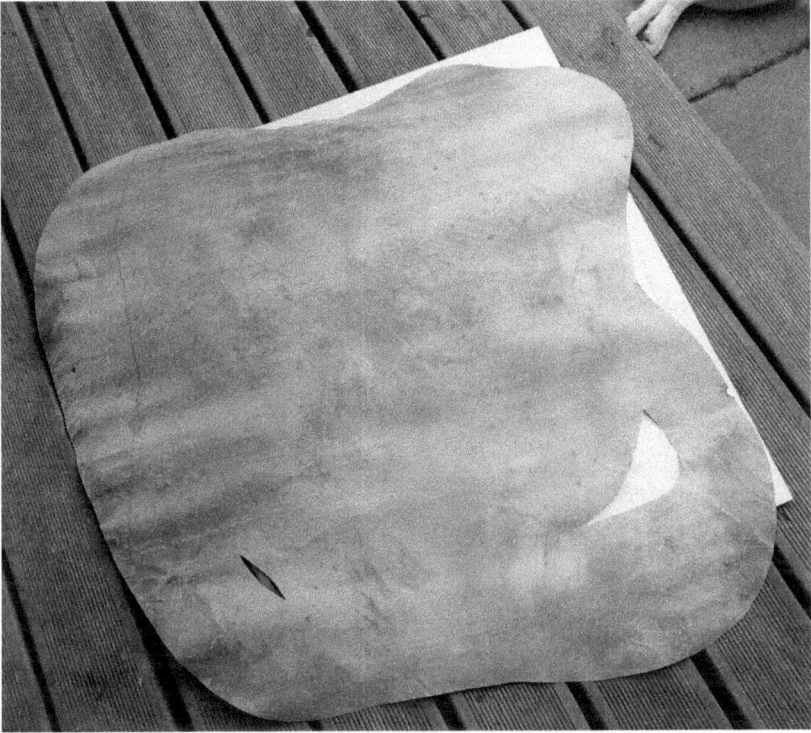

I now get my deer rawhide from **Carbisdale Deerskins** who are the only makers of naturally tanned rawhide I could find. When you get it, there may still be some hairs left on, these can be sanded off very easily. First you need to flatten the hide - reverse fold the hide (as you would a poster to flatten it). Trim the edges and cut around any holes. Please note that deer rawhide is thin enough to cut dry – the hide will not need to be soaked at this stage.

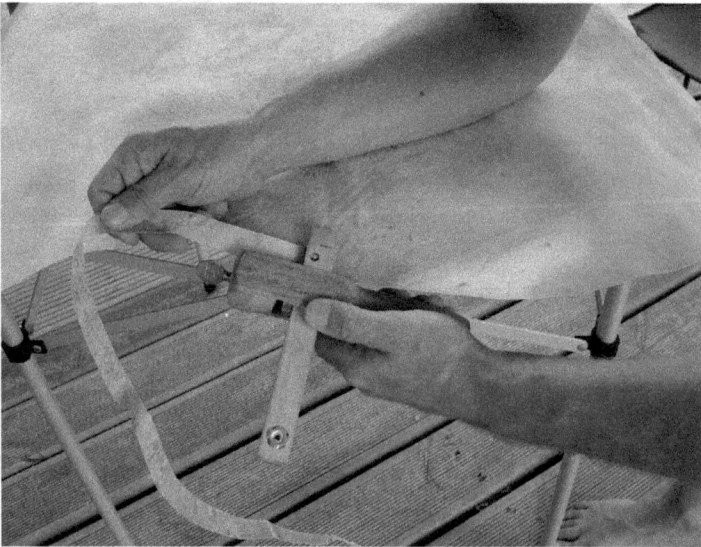

Before cutting with the lace cutter, I find it useful to first cut a short length as shown above left. Also before starting, make sure that the lace

cutter has a new sharp blade fitted. The last photo shows how I progress along making the laces – holding firmly onto the lace and pulling on the lace cutter and using my elbow to keep the rawhide in place.

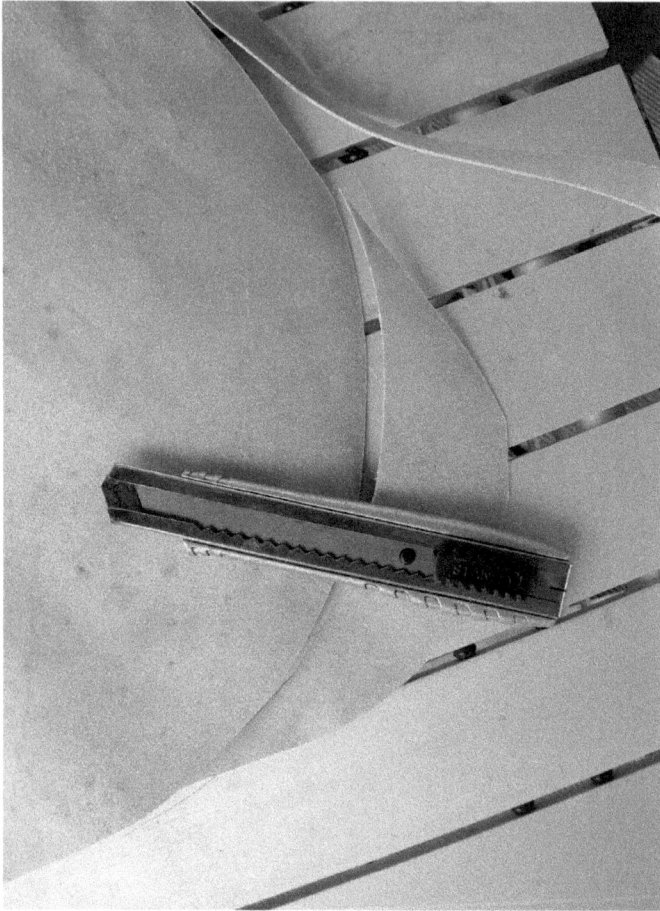

As you progress cutting around the rawhide, the corners will start to get increasingly sharper which will make it harder to keep the lace to a certain width especially along the denser parts of the hide. The photos above show how to cut these to make smoother curves once again – it will mean a certain degree of wastage but it is unavoidable - you will get enough lace for the quiver.

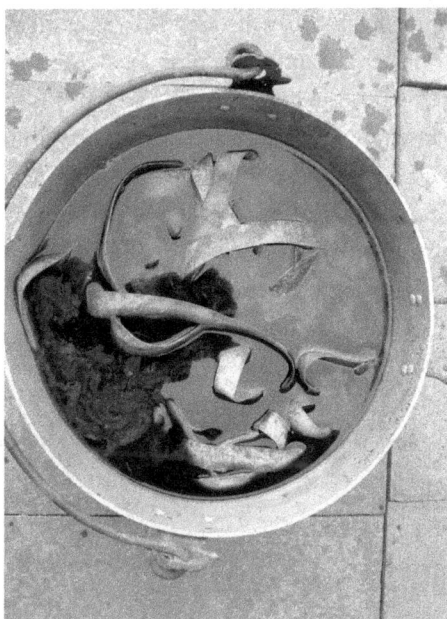

For a 22 inch high quiver you will need 6 lengths of 48 inches long, 1 length of 6 metres for the main braid, plus 3 lengths of 2.6m long. These measurements are on the generous side and once you have cut these lengths, soak the rawhide in warm water for about an hour then hang up as shown on the previous page. The top photo shows me soaking this rawhide in a mixture of black hull powder. I sometimes dye the rawhide to allow the tannins in the dyes I use (grass, bark etc) to colour the hide and depending on the length of time I leave the rawhide in the mixture (1 hour to 1 day) gives the hide some texture and softens it outlook. Remove the lace from the line once it feels like rubber and place into a plastic bag until you need them to prevent them from drying out too much. You will also need a piece 2 inches by 12 ¾ long for the top.

To summarise amounts needed

A hide about 7 ftsq will give you enough lace or lace when they are cut at ¾ inch wide.

You will need;

6 x 48 inches, 3 x 2.6m, 1 x 6m long plus a wide piece of 2 inches x 12 ¾ inches long.

Also cut a length of lace about 1/3 inches wide by 2 ft to lace up the top piece at the end.

After soaking the rawhide place all unused lace into a plastic bag and use it within a week because organic matter, especially from dyes will start to rot the rawhide.

In order to make this quiver, you need a solid form on which to mould the rawhide around. I show here an old round fence post which I cut down in a taper the diameter at the top is 2 ¾ inches wide tapering to 2 inches at the bottom. The whole length of the mould is 26 ½ inches long and the two marks are made at 22 and 24 inches from the bottom. Next use something straight and wide like the length of 20 x 45mm I used to draw two lines down the length of the mould.

The next photos show the mould cut into three pieces. The object of cutting these is to allow easy retrieval of the mould after the rawhide has dried and set – in order to make this easy the two outer pieces are cut at the mark you made at 24 inches leaving the middle piece to extend to the

26 ½ inches. It is also advisable to smooth the cut sides and cover them in some grease or something similar to aid the retrieval of the middle piece. Below right shows the mould taped up and ready to use. You could use anything for the mould as long as it is solid plus could cut it to different shapes just as long as you can remove it from the rawhide afterwards.

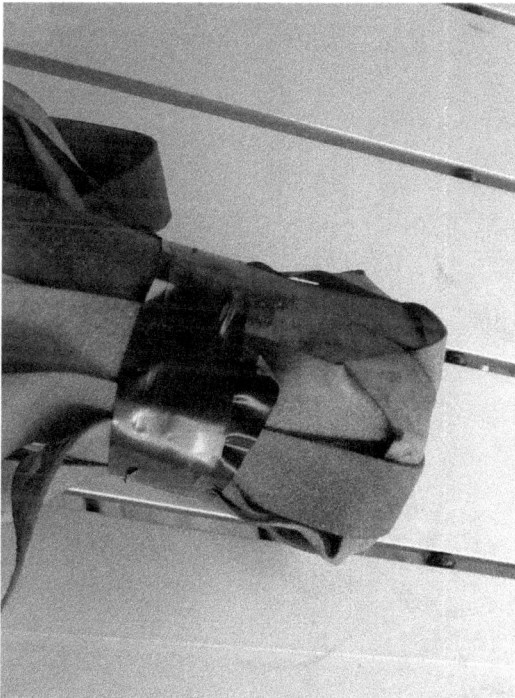

Before laying down or up the 6 x short lengths of rawhide, size a piece of thick leather or other hard material on the bottom of the mould. This is to take the points of the arrows, which would eventually tear the thin rawhide if this is not in place. Above middle shows the 6 lengths of 48 inches marked at their half way points i.e. 24 inches, then braided in an under and over square fashion. Glue the leather piece onto this braid and place over the end of the mould as shown above right, using tape to keep them in place. The braid you will be performing with the 6m long lace i.e. under 1 over 1 will only work with an odd number of vertical lace, so you will only be laying down 11 of the 12 laces shown here, the 1 left over is used to start the braid but for now lay it down as you do the others as it will aid tightening the others into place.

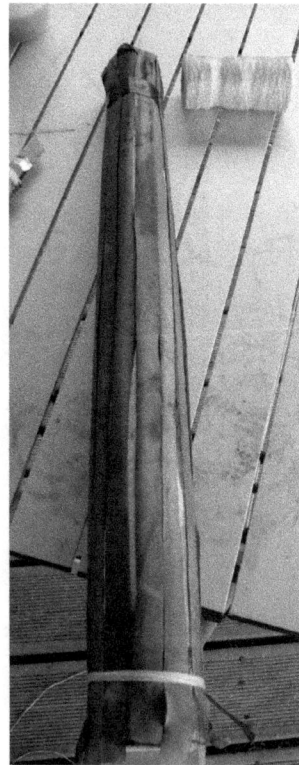

Laying down the vertical laces involves gently pulling each of the 12 laces at a time to just beyond the 22 inch mark and fixing it into place using artificial sinew or any other thread available. Once they are all in place, pull harder on each of them making them tight and fix more thread into place above the first lot to hold all of them in place. Remove the lower amounts of thread and the 12th lace at this point. Above right shows me winding the long 6m piece around the whole mould to check that there is enough.

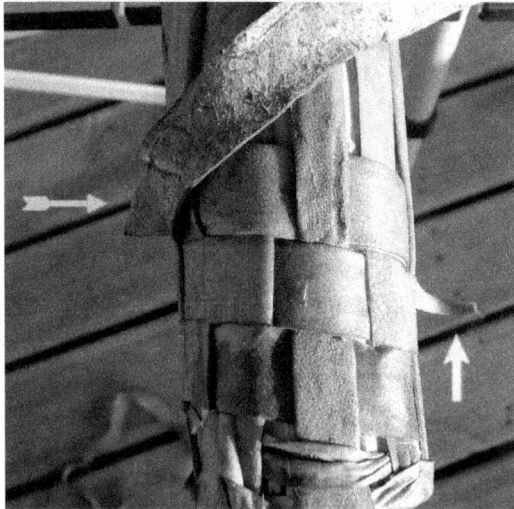

To start the main braid take the 12th lace left over from the step above and braid under 1, over 1 and so on as shown above. Carry on until you reach the end of that lace, then start braiding with the longer lace at least 3 unders before the end of the shorter lace. Above right shows the blue arrow point at the end of the shorter lace and the white arrow points to the start of the longer lace. As you braid up wards remember to remove the tape used to keep the mould pieces together.

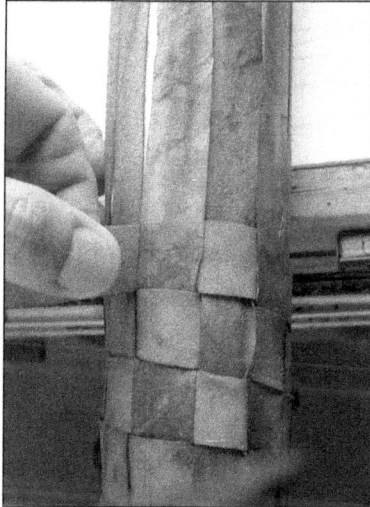

As you braid, some of the vertical laces may still be quite wet and tend to fold up as you pull the longer lace through them. I braided a series of 3

unders and overs at a time and upon pulling the whole length through, gently pushed the longer lace down onto the lower braid while also flattening out the vertical lace just worked. You may tend to form some gaps depending on the difference in the laces width but this is OK just as long as they are not wide.

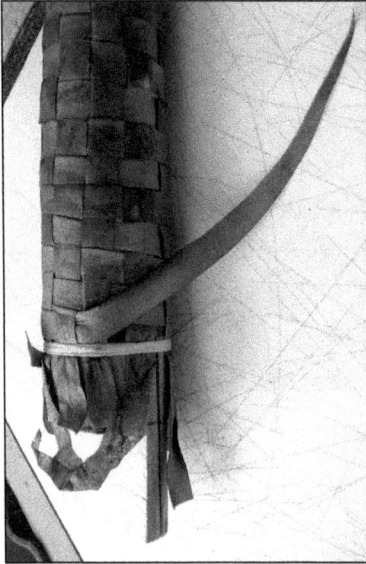

Upon reaching near the top, narrow the lace to a point (above left) and carry on braiding pushing the lace under the thread if needs be until the end is reached (above right).

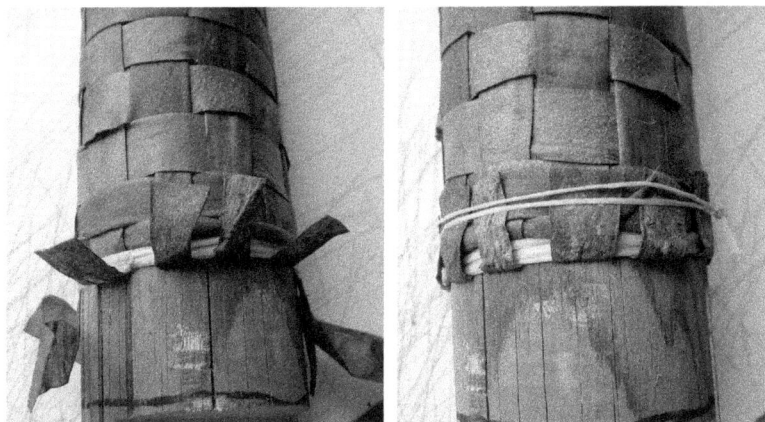

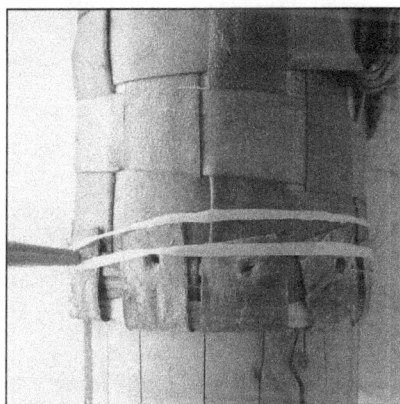

Last stage is to bend the ends of the vertical laces over the thread, then cut to leave about 4/5 inch left. Tie these into place using thread (above middle), then using a sharp pointed tool makes holes in each - this is to aid in sewing on the top.

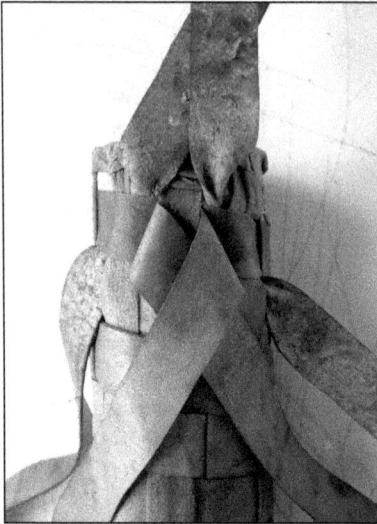

Next stage is to start the shoulder strap. I start mine at the bottom of the quiver, take the 3 x 2.6m lengths of rawhide and feed through the braid of the quiver as shown above left using an awl to push them through if needed. Pull each until you have an equal amount of lace either side. The braid for the shoulder strap is the same as for the quiver i.e. under 1, over 1. Start by crossing all the laces on the left over to the right and vice versa with those on the right to the left ensuring the right unders and overs match up then leading with the higher lace continue with the under 1 over 1 braid sequence

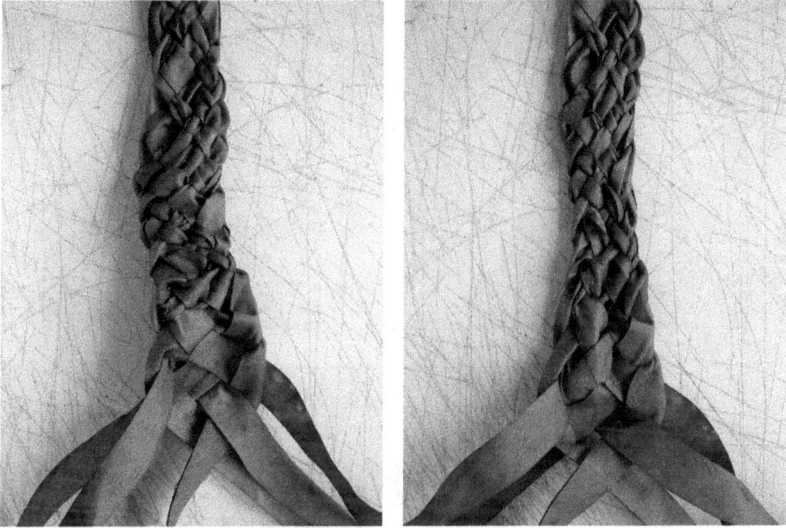

As you braid these wide thin pieces of rawhide, it will be impossible to stop them bunching up (above left) and at some point it may seem as if you won't be able to make a long enough shoulder strap (I was aiming for 32 inches). However, you will find that the lace will stretch quite a bit when pulled (above right). So after awhile of braiding pull and carry on doing this until you have reached the length you need. You could pull the lace until it is very narrow but I prefer some width to mine.

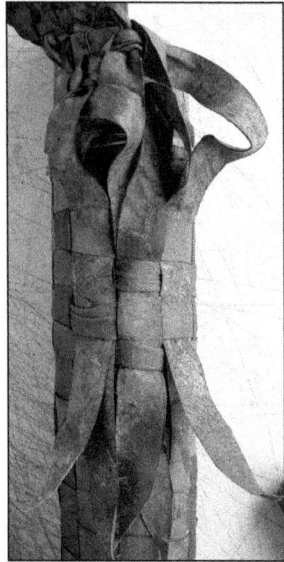

To end the shoulder strap, divide the 6 into 3 sets of two (above left) then thread these pairs about 2 inches from the top of the quiver back into the braid of the quiver making sure that you use the verticals laces that match up with those you started with. First place all three sets loosely through two unders (above middle), then tighten (above right). Lastly hang up the quiver and leave to dry. Once it is dry snip off the ends of these laces and tuck in.

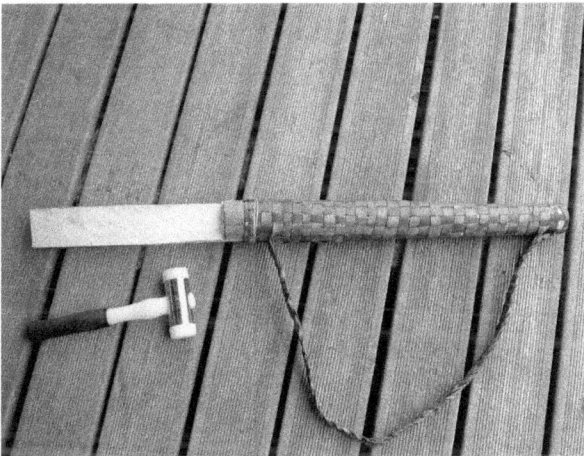

First photo show how to hang up the quiver ensuring that it does not touch anything as this may hinder patches of it drying. Once dry the rawhide has tightened up and pressed the mould together to such an extent that a hammer maybe needed to extract it from the quiver. Once the middle is out the two outer pieces should just come out easily.

To cut the rawhide for the top, I just cut it from the dry spare piece of rawhide to the width of the ruler above or 2 inches wide by 12 4/3 inches long then soak in water for ½ hour. If you cut and soak this the same time as the laces, ensure to keep it in a plastic bag, for no longer than a week as mould will start to grow on it especially if you soaked it in dye – an organic material.

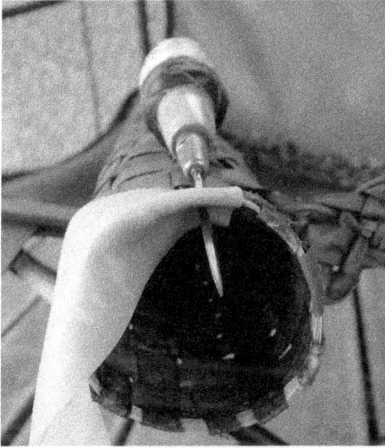

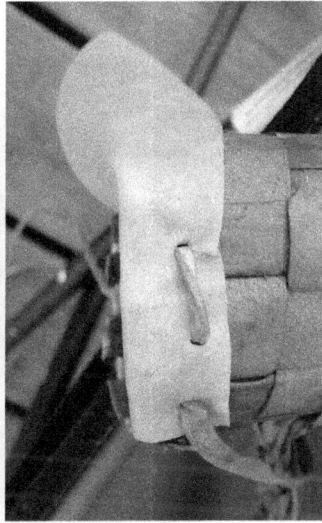

Starting where ever you like, use a sharp awl to pouch the top rawhide to create the sewing holes – I found it best to make these holes as I sewed. Sew right around the outer diameter in and out, then go round again finishing off the sewing pattern as shown above right – cut the lace on the outside of the quiver and hang up to dry again.

The last job is to coat the quiver with varnish – I used to use yacht varnish but it takes too long to dry so now put about three coats of this fast drying varnish onto it. In the end they both do the same job of stiffening up the quiver and making it water proof. To aid water proofing the shoulder lace I coat that with Aussie conditioner or any wax coating will do to make it at least resistant to moisture.

Making a braided Knife handle and sheath

I will be covering two types of braiding; the short knots of the knife handle ends being quite recognisable as pineapple knots.

The braiding along the handle could also be done as a longer pineapple knot but I used a method created by the Gaucho cowboys of the pampas from Argentina. Called fid work, the gauchos have and do create handle covers of such fine lace that it is hard to tell that it is braided using upto and above 100 strings on handles just like the one below. I have only used 32 on this one but any number of laces can be used.

In this section I cover; Lace prep, Handle foundation, Fid work, Braid pattern aid, Tools and equipment, pineapple knots; 9 parts, 8 bight – 13 parts, 12 bight, Placement of knots and lastly knot foundation.

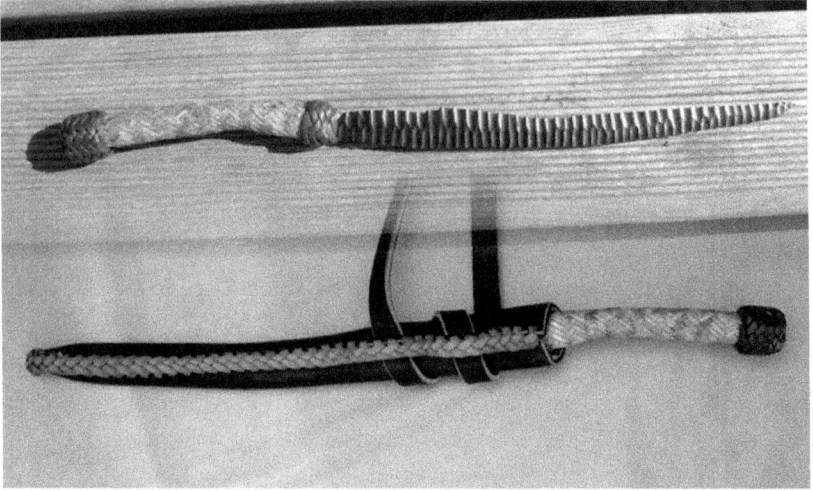

Quite an unusual knife created for a black set of armour.

Close up of the fid work and two pineapple knots.

Prep of rawhide lace

First off for this type and any type of braiding, don't use bought lace. In most cases it is made from bleached rawhide which weakens it and it is thick, but the good news is that making your own is not hard and will in the long run cost less. Bought leather lace is fine for the small knots although it can be made the same way rawhide is from a hide.

Rawhide is better cut when damp which you do by immersing it into warm water then placing into a plastic bag and leaving over night, this gives the water time to soak throughout the hide. Then remove and allow drying till it regains firmness slightly and feels like paper rather than a soggy mass.

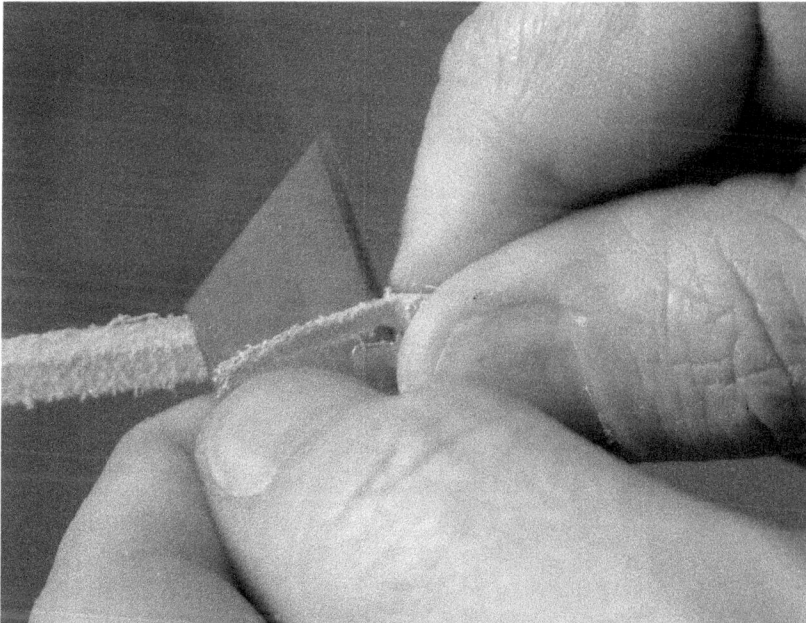

For fid work you only need short lengths of lace, so you start by cutting wide strips out of the hide, stretch and run through a splitter to even out the thickness of the hide but this is not necessary if you have not got one. Next use a lace cutter like Tandy sales or do by hand and cut the lace to the width you need for the job. Rawhide and leather lace should be bevelled from the underside (as shown above and below) in order to produce a smooth finish to the fid work but it is duffercult on lace that is fine and narrow and mistakes cause uneven lace as shown in my work. Place lace back into plastic bag while not being used and if during lacing the rawhide becomes too dry and stiff, re-soak with a sponge. Leather lace should be coated in leather conditioner to prevent too much friction when braiding.

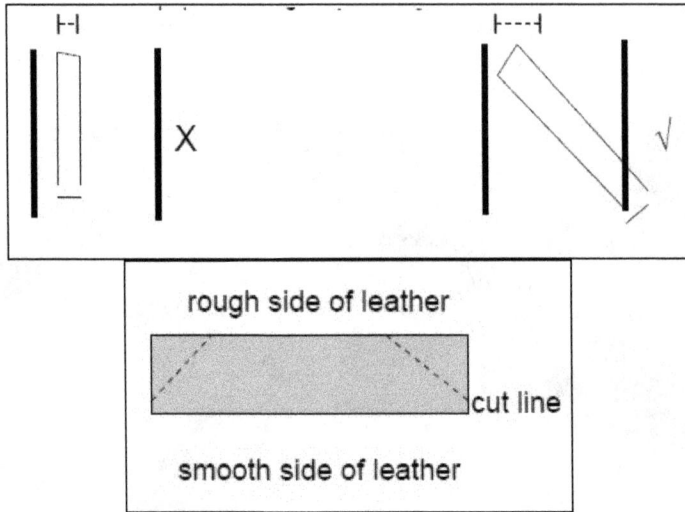

To find the amount of lace needed to cover any sized core, I normally lay the lace against the core as shown below at an angle corresponding to how it will lay once braided. If you're good with maths then there are ways to work it out that way but I am more comfortable using this method.

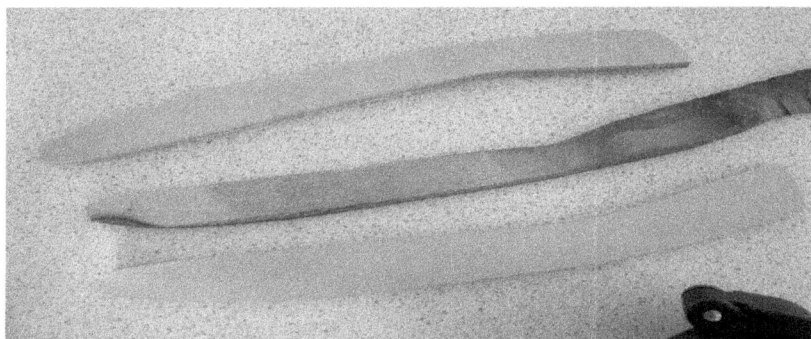

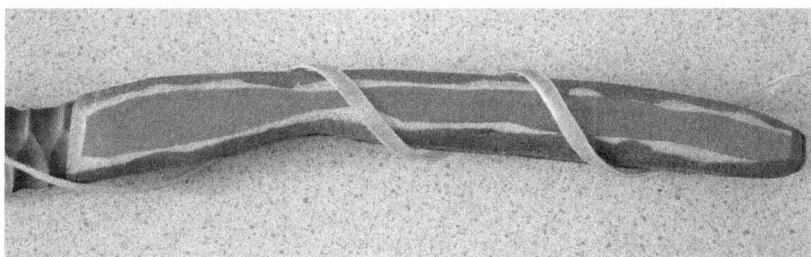

Onto the full tang of this knife, I cut out two pieces of 6mm leather to cover both sides of the metal and glued on with epoxy glue. After 15 minutes I trimmed the sides and top to make a more rounded handle profile then coated in saddle soap. After finding the amount of lace I needed to cover the handle I then wrapped one lace around the handle descending at a 45 degree angle to find the length needed. This would also aid in finding out how many turns would be needed if an extended pineapple knot was being used.

To start the fid work, one side of the lace has to be applied to the handle as shown above. This can be duffercult trying to lay 16 lace all at the same time. To aid this I first apply glue to the top of the handle and the ends of each lace, once these were on then used a constrictor knot to keep them in place. If using lots of strings narrower then 2mm, wind artificial string around the end securing one lace every turn, this also starts a good foundation for an end knot. Next, slowly twist the lace around the handle ensuring that each lies even, this can be helped by applying elastic bands down the handle as you lay the lace. It is not easy doing this part but doable, just take your time. Once you have finished, tie off the end and carefully pull each lace to tighten them up.

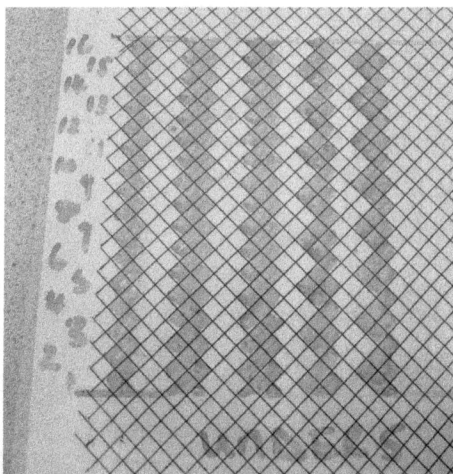

As mentioned earlier, the patterns possible in fib work are limitless, for this example I just used a simple under 3, over 3 sequences leading to a short section of under 2, over 3 and under 3, over 2. As shown above left, above right shows an example I have used in whip handles as shown on simple graph paper covered in plastic. In most cases a simple pattern of under 3, over 3 is enough for fid work and complex patterns don't really show up as they would if using coloured leather lace.

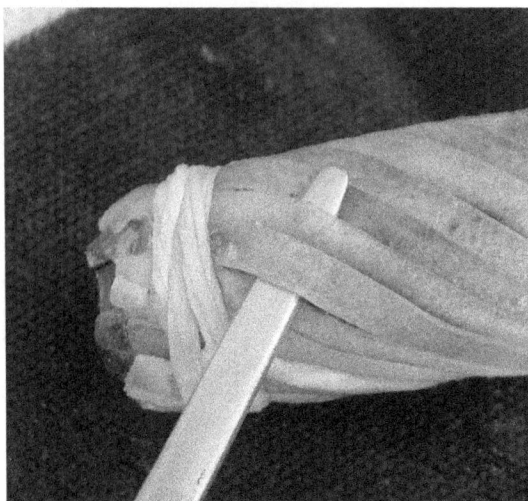

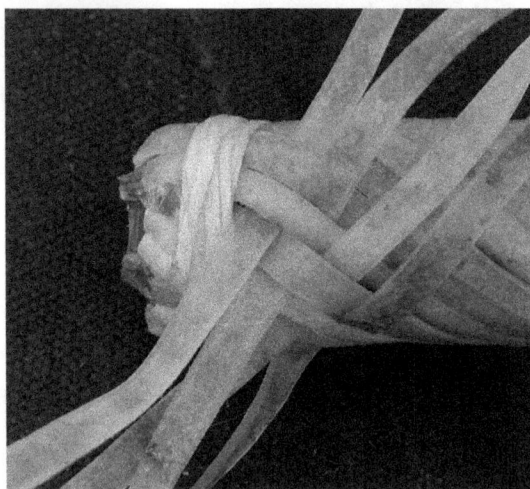

Start by first applying a two prong needle to the end of each lace, it is not totally necessary to attach needles but I find it makes the job a whole lot easier. Then using an awl lift up the first two laces as shown above and start staggering each lace under 2 as shown above right.

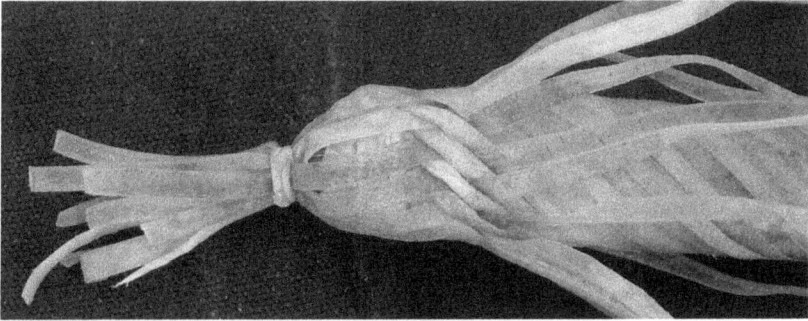

This shows the first complete run of lace, notice how they are positioned at 45 degree angle. From here on in it is just a case of braiding each lace at the same 45 degree angle under 3 over 3 down the length of the handle.

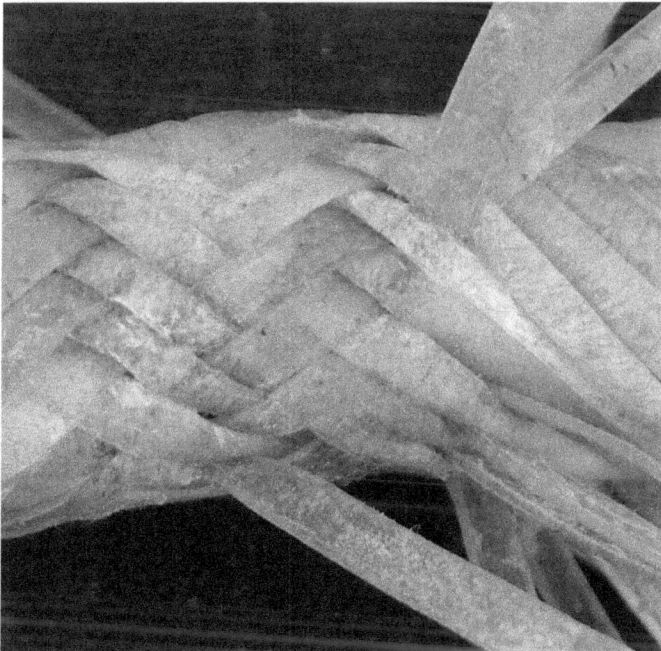

Above left shows a typical problem that is encountered at the end of each run, whereby you may find that there is not enough room to fit in the last lace – all you do here is go around all the other laces making sure that they are tight up against one another and at the right angle. As you do place each lace, make sure that they are tight up against one another to not only ensure that they fit but this also ensures that each pattern you create is even and not lop-sided. Above right shows an example where the lace has twisted, all you have to do here is remove the needle, pull the lace back, re-attach the needle and thread under again.

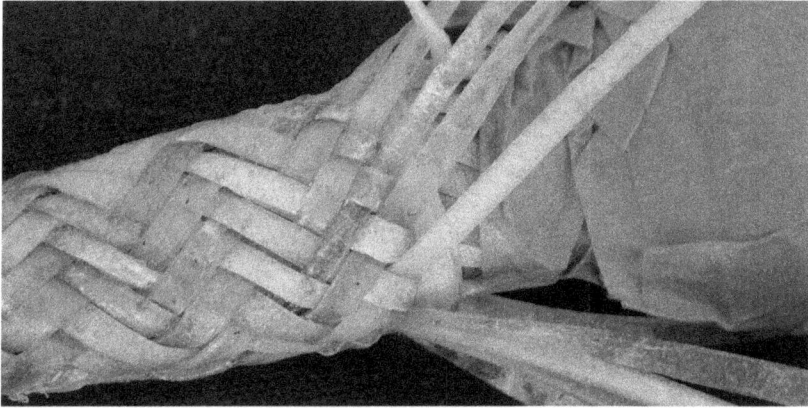

This photo show how best to end the braiding ensuring that you end it with an under. Once finished, tighten all the lace you have just braided and those underneath.

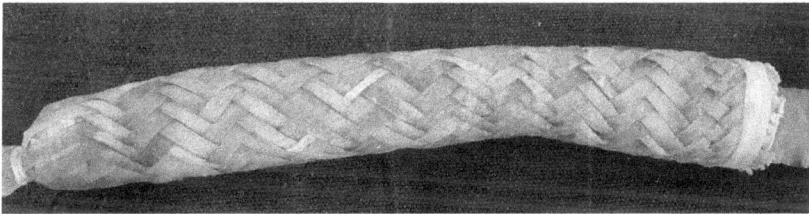

Here is the fid work on the handle complete with both ends tied off.

Braided Knots

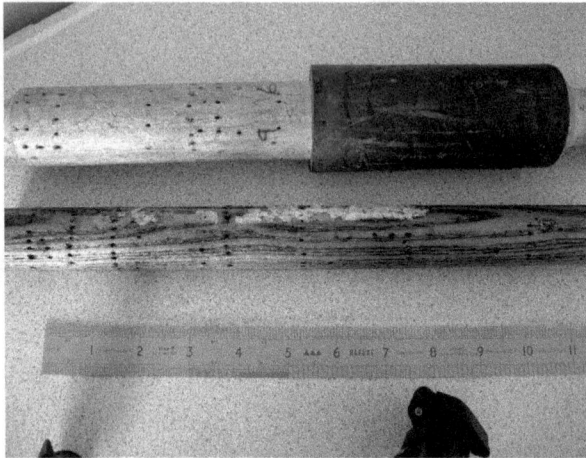

Here is displayed the pieces I use to first do my braided knots on – could use any circular implement but I guess I just got used to using a kitchen rolling pin and an old broom handle – holes in them are from countless use. Above right shows my scratch awl and braiding awl plus pliers, needles and nails.

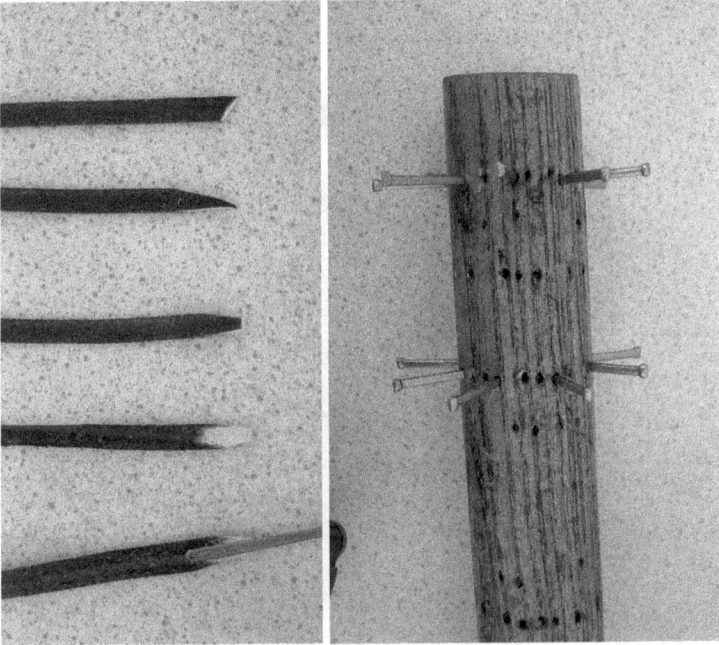

Shown here are the stages in cutting the end of lace for a two prong needle, from top to bottom – cut to a point, snip off end (ensuring the end is no wider than the needle), then bevel underside, slip into needle ensuring the prongs go into the smooth side of the leather and close with a pair of pliers. Above middle shows arrangement of nails for the 12 bight knot (meaning 12 nails on top and 12 on bottom) spaced roughly an inch further apart then the length of knot needed. The next photo shows all the laced wrapped around all the nails and is a good way to tell if you have enough lace for the job before starting.

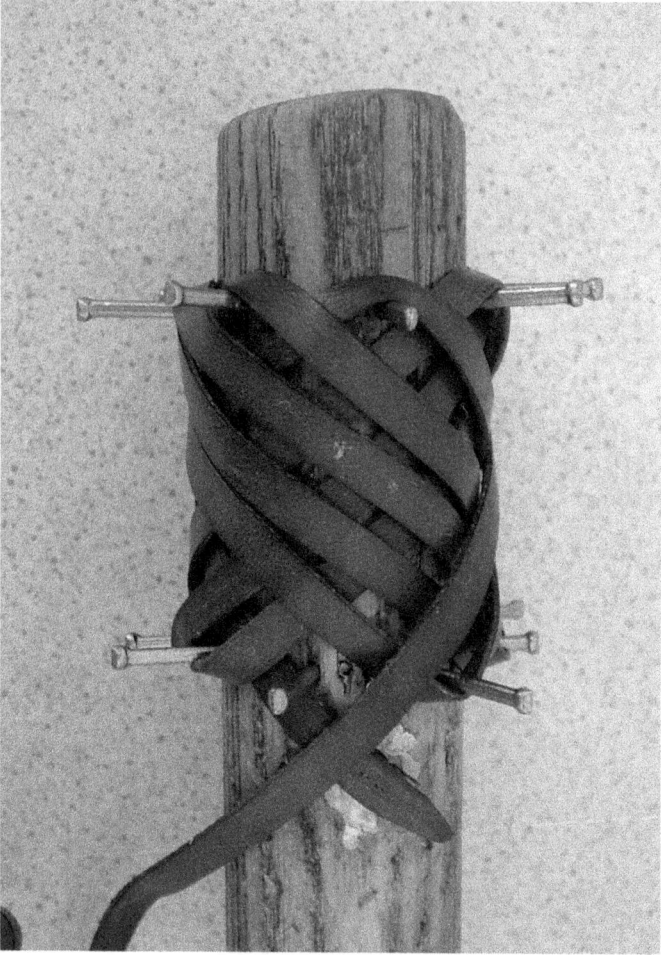

Perfect Pineapple Knots

The perfect pineapple is just like the normal pineapple, i.e. it creates a knot with a herringbone pattern, but the perfect pineapple is made from only one lace whereas normally it is made up of two Turks heads interwoven together.

To help hide the ends of the fid work on this knife handle, I used two – the 9 part, 8 bights and the 13 parts, 12 bight.

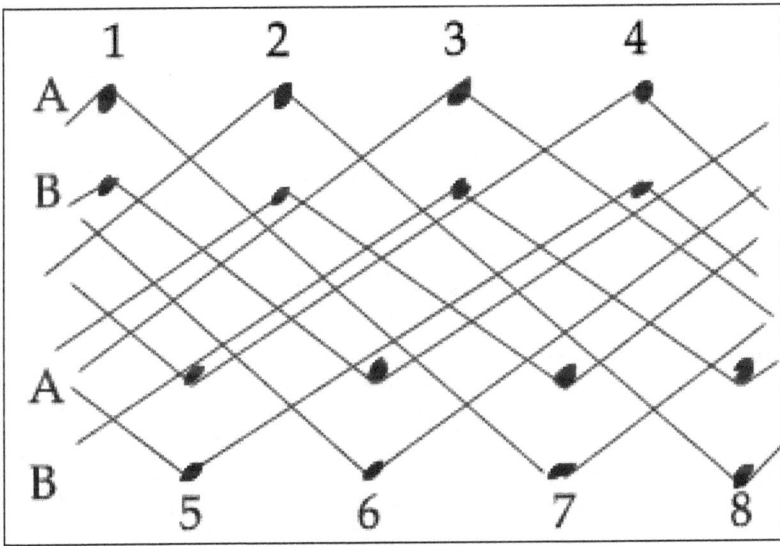

Above is a diagram of the arrangement of nails needed for the 9 part, 8 bight knot. The number of bights always indicates how many nails you need but with this knot two sets of 8 nails are needed. Please notice that the top and bottom nails are slightly off centre to one another.

Following these number above it should be easy to create this knot from the instructions below;

Up 8B, clear run, to 2A, Down, under 1, to 7A

Up 7A, clear run, to 2B, Down, over 1, to 7B

Up 7B, over 1, under 1, to 1A, Down, over 2, under 1, to 6A

Up 6A, under 2, to 1B, Down, under 1, over 2, to 6B

Up 6B, under 1, over 2, under 1, to 4A, Down, under 2, over 2, under 1, to 5A

Up 5A, over 2, under 2, to 4B, Down, over 1, under 2, over 2, to 5B

Up 5B, over 1, under 2, over 2, under 1, to 3A, Down, over 2, under 2, over 2, under 1, to 8A

Up 8A, under 2, over 2, under 2, to 3B, Down, under 1, over 2, under 2, over 2, to 8B

Up 8B, under 1, over 2, under 2 (do this extra to help tie off knot).

Finished 9 part, 8 bight knot with nails removed.

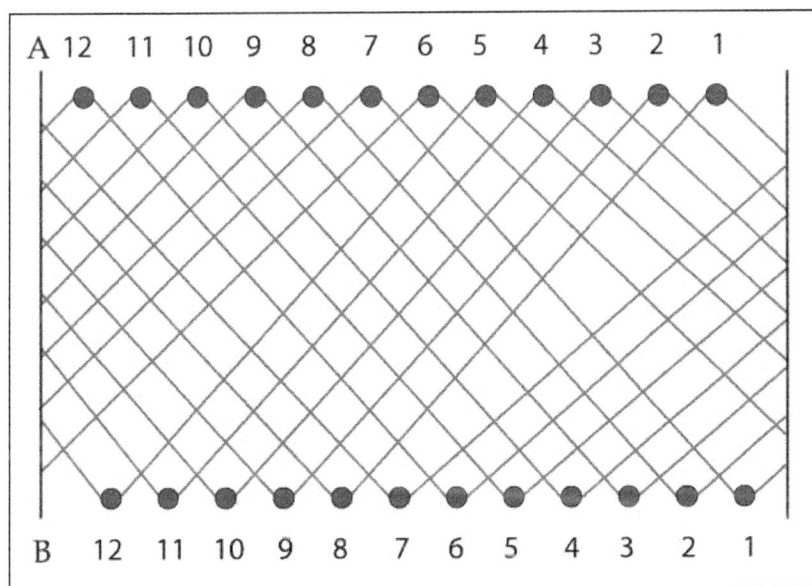

Above is the diagram for the 13 part, 12 bight knot – the only difference is that there is only two circles of nails this time instead of four

1. Up 1B, clear run, to 7A, Down, over 1, to 2B
2. Up 2B, over 1, to 8A, Down, under 2, to 3B
3. Up 3B, over 1, under 1, to 9A, Down, under 1, over 2, to 4B
4. Up 4B, under 2, over 1, to 10A, Down, over 2, under 2, to 5B
5. Up 5B, under 1, over 2, under 1, to 11A, Down, over 1, under 2,
6. over 2 to 6B
7. Up 6B, over 2, under 2, over 1, to 12A, Down, under 2, over 2,
8. under 2, to 7B
9. Up 7B, over 1, under 2, over 2, under 1, to 1A, Down, under 1,
10. over 2, under 2, over 2, to 8B
11. Up 8B, under 2, over 2, under 2, over 1, to 2A, Down, over 2,
12. under 2, over 2, under 2, to 9B
13. Up 9B   under 1, over 2, under 2, over 2, under 1   to 3A
14. Down 3A over 1, under 2, over 2, under 2, over 2   to 10B
15. Up 10B over 2, under 2, over 2, under 2, over 1   to 4A
16. Down 4A under 2, over 2, under 2, over 2, under 2   to 11B
17. Up 11B   over 1, under 2, over 2, under 2, over 2, under 1   to 5A
18. Down 5A under 1, over 2, under 2, over 2, under 2,. Over 1   to 12B
19. Up 12B under 2, over 2, under 2, over 2, under 2, over 1   to 6A
20. Down 6A   over 2, under 2, over 2, under 2, over 2, under 2 to 1B
21. Up 1B, under 1, over 2, under 2 (over the first lace to help tie the knot).

here are the two knot finished on the wooden forms, (left 8 bights, right 12 bights). Once all the nails are removed I normally tighten them up on the form and then tighten up again on a smaller form if needed, after that it is a case of tightening them up on the job.

The purpose of a knots foundation is to keep the knot in place as solid as possible and give it form. The smaller 8 bight knot did not need a big foundation as displayed above for the 12 bight, for the 8 I merely wound some artificial sinew around the end of the handle on which the knot was placed and tightened. The foundation is a much securer way to attach a knot as it is nailed into the whole job ensuring that the knot will not loosen over time and turn.

Examples of fid work on a walking stick from coloured leather lace.

Resources

Supplies;

Tandy leather factory – stores all over the world for tools and leather/rawhide.

Ebay – There are numerous outlets selling here now.

Books;

Ron Edwards excellent leather craft books

Encyclopedia of rawhide and leather braiding – Bruce Grant – probably one of the best and most well accessible books on the subject (link is to amazon.co.uk)

Forums;

Australian plaiters and whipmakers association – Whipmakers and braider from around the world.

Leather workers – Global leathercraft forum covering all aspects leather work.